I0541654

www.ingramcontent.com/pod-product-compliance
Lightning Source LLC
Chambersburg PA
CBHW041615120626
46551CB00002B/452

9798992918120

Learn Colors With Animals

تَعَلَّمُ الأَلْوَان

مَعَ الحَيَوَانَاتِ

Safa Adam

صفاء آدم

Hello, little friends! Did you know animals come in amazing colors? In this book, we'll learn colors with beautiful and exciting animals! Are you ready for fun?

Dedication

To my beloved children,
Ahmed, Salih, Noor, and Omer,
This book is for you—my little stars who fill my days with joy and laughter. May these colorful animals spark your curiosity, brighten your world, and make learning as fun as your playful hearts.
With all my love,💖

"Every color holds a story, and every animal a friend. May you explore them all with wonder!"

أَبْيَضُ

White

الخَرُوفُ أَيَضُ
The sheep is white

مُنفوشٌ وَدَافِئٌ
Fluffy and warm!

أَصْفَرُ

Yellow

الْكُتْكُوتُ أَصْفَرُ

The chick is yellow

نَاعِمٌ وَمُنْفُوشٌ

Soft and fluffy!

أَحْمَرُ

Red

الخُنْفُسَاءُ حَمْرَاءُ
The ladybug is red

مُسَاعِدَةٌ ومُنَقَّطَةُ
Spotted and helper

أَزْرَقٌ

Blue

السَّمَكَةُ زَرْقَاءُ

The fish is blue

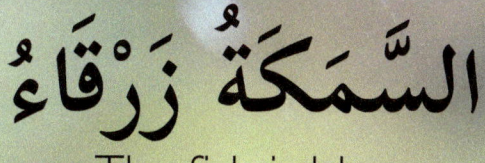

زَلِقةٌ وَنَاعِمة

Slippery and smooth!

أَخْضَرُ

Green

السَّلْحَفَاةُ خَضْرَاءُ

The turtle is green

بَطِيئَةٌ وَقَوِيَّةٌ

Slow and strong!

بُرْتُقَالِيٌّ

Orange

الثَّعْلَبُ بُرْتُقَالِيٌّ

The fox is orange

سَرِيعٌ وَذَكِيٌّ

Fast and clever!

بَنَفْسَجِيٌّ

Purple

الفَرَاشَةُ بَنَفْسَجِيَّةٌ

The butter fly is purple

خَفِيفَةٌ وَتَرْفُرِفُ

Light and fluttery!

بُنِّيّ

Brown

الدُّبُّ بُنِّيٌّ

The bear is brown

كَبِيرٌ وَثَقِيلٌ

Big and heavy

وَرْدِيَّ

Pink

الْخِنْزِيرُ وَرْدِيٌّ

The pig is pink

مُدَوَّرٌ وَيَتَلَوَّى

Round and wiggly!

أَسْوَدُ

Black

اَلْقِطُّ أَسْوَدُ

The cat is black

ناعِمٌ وَجَمِيلٌ

Soft and cute

Design and layout by Safa Adam

First Edition: 2025

Self-Published by Safa Adam

ISBN: 979-8-9929181-2-0